£7.50

Contents

Levels*	Title	Composer	Page
P G	Hot Hot Hot	Alphonsus Cassell, arr. Charles Beale	3
P G	Bossa Brasileiro	Alan Haughton	6
P G	She Will Be Loved	Maroon 5, arr. Nancy Litten	8
P P	Calm Waters	Alan Bullard	10
P P	Lamento	Andrew Eales	12
P P	Rolling Down to Rio	Mike Cornick	14
P P	Summer Samba	Mike Cornick	16
P G (G)	Dancing in the Moonlight	Sherman Kelly, arr. John Caudwell	19
P P (G)	Satin Doll	Duke Ellington, arr. Derek Hobbs	22
P (P) P	King of the Road	Roger Miller, arr. Nancy Litten	25
P G (G)(G)	Fudged	Andrew Eales after J. S. Bach	28
P P (G)(G)	Don't Get Around Much Anymore	Duke Ellington, arr. Mike Cornick	30

* G = gold; P = platinum; ( ) = the line must be played but cannot be assessed for a Medal.

Hot Hot Hot

Alphonsus Cassell
arr. Charles Beale

Bossa Brasileiro

Alan Haughton

AB 3225

She Will Be Loved

Maroon 5
arr. Nancy Litten

Music by Adam Levine, James Valentine, Jesse Carmichael, Mickey Madden & Ryan Dusick
© Copyright 2002 February Twenty Second Music, USA
Universal Music Publishing MGB Limited
Used by permission of Music Sales Limited
All Rights Reserved. International Copyright Secured.

AB 3225

Calm Waters

Alan Bullard

　　　　AB 3225

pan flute

Lamento

Andrew Eales

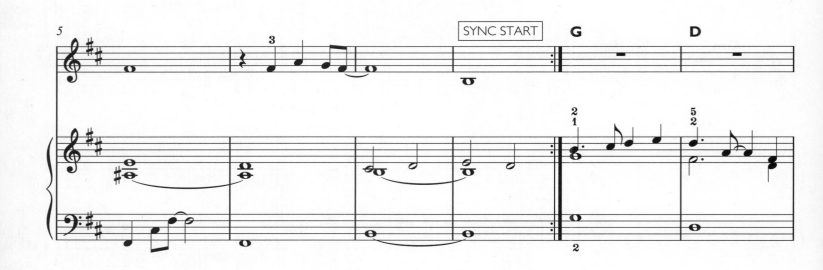

AB 3225

Rolling Down to Rio

Mike Cornick

AB 3225

Summer Samba

Mike Cornick

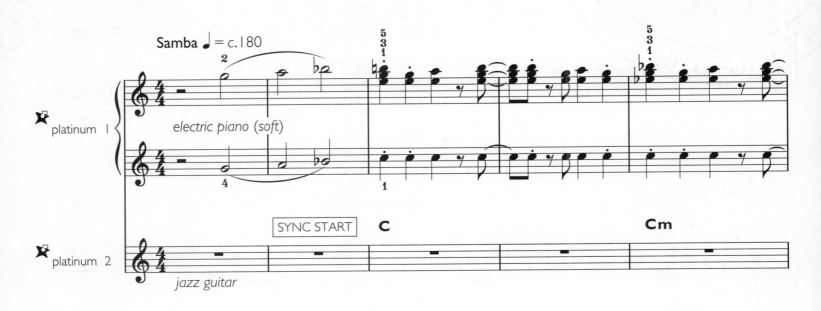

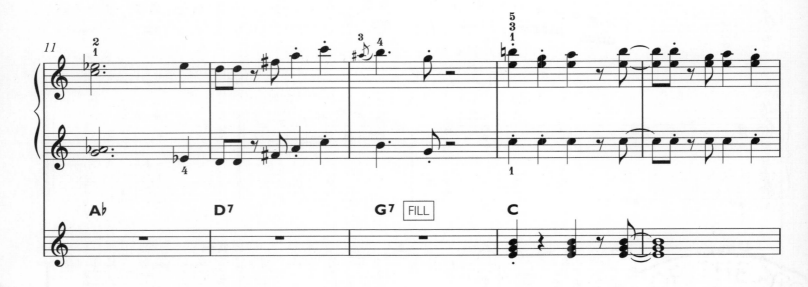

Dancing in the Moonlight

Sherman Kelly
arr. John Caudwell

Satin Doll

Duke Ellington
arr. Derek Hobbs

King of the Road

Roger Miller
arr. Nancy Litten

Fudged

Andrew Eales after J. S. Bach

AB 3225

Don't Get Around Much Anymore

Duke Ellington
arr. Mike Cornick